SUPERMAN™
SCIENCE

THE REAL-WORLD SCIENCE BEHIND SUPERMAN'S POWERS

BY *AGNIESZKA BISKUP* AND *TAMMY ENZ*

SUPERMAN CREATED BY
JERRY SIEGEL
AND **JOE SHUSTER**
BY SPECIAL ARRANGEMENT
WITH THE JERRY SIEGEL FAMILY

Capstone Young Readers
a capstone imprint

Published by Capstone Young Readers
A Capstone Imprint
1710 Roe Crest Drive
North Mankato, Minnesota 56003
www.mycapstone.com

STAR38102

Library of Congress Cataloging-in-Publication Data is available on the Library of Congress website.

ISBN: 978-1-62370-702-6 (paperback)

Summary: Superman is the World's Greatest Hero! With super-strength, lightning speed, laser vision, and the ability to fly, he keeps Earth safe. But what is the science behind strength, speed, sight, and flight? And does anything or anyone in our world have similar abilities to Superman? Superman Science explores how real-life science and engineering relate to the Man of Steel's famous powers—and the real-world connections may surprise you.

Editorial Credits
Editor: Kristen Mohn
Designer: Bob Lentz
Production Specialist: Tori Abraham
Media Researcher: Eric Gohl

Photo Credits
Dreamstime: Chrisstanley, 79, Denys Hliuza-smykovskyi, 126; **DVIDS:** NASA, 81, 102, SSgt. Jonathan Snyder, 34b; **iStockphoto:** ByronD, 96, Dirk Ott, 117, oguzaral, 112, Peter Burnett, 52t, pidjoe, 127b, Pieter De Pauw, 137t, ShaneKato, 57b, Vasily Smirnov, 36; **Library of Congress:** 10, 14 all, 71; **NARA:** 15; **NASA:** 13, 37, 54, 55t, 85 all, 87b, 91, 103, 104, 105, Bill Ingalls, 87t, DFRC/X-43A Development Team, 83, JPL-Caltech, 55b, JSC, 12, Tony Landis, 33t; **Shutterstock:** aeiddam, 61b, AkeSak, 51mr, Al Mueller, 25b, Aleksei Lazukov, 17t, Alessandro De Maddalena, 97b, Alexandra Lande, 16, Alexey U, 29, alphaspirit, 128, Andre Coetzer, 93, Andrew Bignell, 131b, Andrey Khachatryan, 33b, Antonio Gravante, 73, Aphelleon, 77t, Artyom Anikeev, 89b, Attila Jandi, 24, BasPhoto, 127t, Betto Rodrigues, 19, Boykov, 31b, Carolina K. Smith MD, 51tr, cbpix, 61t, ChameleonsEye, 78, chombosan, 139, Christian Mueller, 11b, chungking, 108, CreativeHQ, 67, CWA Studios, 69t, D. Kucharski K. Kucharska, 51tl, Dan Simonsen, 38, dangdumrong, 123, Daniel Huebner, 22, Dario Sabljak, 51ml, 64r, Dennis W. Donohue, 58, Designua, 42, 47, 111t, 114, Digital Storm, cover mr, 89t, digitalbalance, 135b, Dirk Ercken, 28, Donjiy, 59, dotshock, 118, dwphotos, 119b, eddtoro, 18, Eduard Kyslynskyy, 132b, Ensuper, 6, Erik Zandboer, 131t, Ery Azmeer, 136, Evgeny Karandaev, 59 bkg, Fedorov Oleksiy, 106b, FloridaStock, 9b, ForeverLee, 113b, Fotokostic, 77b, FotoLoveCamera, 39, Gui Jun Peng, 74, Guido Akster, back cover tr, 60, Harvepino, 99t, Henrik Larsson, 135t, holbox, 53b, 119t, Image Point Fr, 64l, 72, itsmejust, cover tr, 68b, 69b, James Steidl, 133b, Janossy Gergely, 92b, Jari Sokka, 26t, Jochen Kost, 84, Joe Belanger, 137b, Joe_Potato, 11t, Jonathan C Photography, back cover bl, 92t, Joseph Sohm, 130, Kaliva, 101b, Kasza, 70, KITSANANAN, 62b, Komsan Loonprom, 116, Kovaleva_Ka, 46, koya979, 20, Krasowit, 90, lafayette-picture, 51b, Lee Yiu Tung, 23r, LifetimeStock, 122, Lu Yao, 35, Luiscar74, 121b, Marianne Taylor, 62t, Mariia Tagirova, 27, martan, 113t, Maximus256, 53t, MCarter, 94, Mmaxer, 43, MO_SES Premium, 86, Monkey Business Images, 107, muratart, cover bl, back cover tl, 9t, Nature Art, 133t, Nerthuz, 111b, Nightman1965, 66, OPIS Zagreb, 32, OZMedia, 68t, Pal2iyawit, 125l, pan demin, 57t, Peter Hermes Furian, 44, 48, 49t, Peter Vrabel, 26b, PHOTOCREO Michal Bednarek, 129t, PhotoStock10, 97t, possohh, 65, Richard Whitcombe, 134, Robert Przybysz, 49b, Roy Pedersen, 129b, Ryan M. Bolton, 23bl, Sandra Matic, 63, sciencepics, 106t, Sergey Nivens, 40, Sindre T, 17b, snapgalleria, 45, Solis Images, 88, Starover Sibiriak, 56, Stefano Cavoretto, cover tl, back cover br, 120, Steve Byland, cover br, 95, stihii, 115t, SVSimagery, 82, Todd Shoemake, 98, Tony Campbell, 23tl, valeriiaarnaud, 52b, Vereshchagin Dmitry, 140, Ververidis Vasilis, 125r, vitstudio, 115b, Volina, 21, Volodymyr Burdiak, 132t, Waldemarus, 80, wavebreakmedia, 50, Werner Lehmann, 25t, Yeko Photo Studio, 121t, Zzvet, 141; **USAF:** 31t, TSgt. Effrain Lopez, 34t, TSgt. Michael Haggerty, 30; **USGS:** 99b; **Wikimedia:** Axion23, 100, Bri Ham, 101t

TABLE OF CONTENTS

RO447918167

THE SCIENCE OF SUPERMAN

Superman may be the most famous super hero of all time. Who doesn't know his origin story? Sent to Earth as a baby from the dying planet Krypton. Raised in Kansas as an ordinary human by Jonathan and Martha Kent. But this hero is far from ordinary. As an alien from another planet, Superman has all sorts of powers that we can only dream about. Superman's not only fast and strong (he's not called the Man of Steel for nothing), but he also flies, is incredibly smart, and has super-vision.

As ordinary humans, we can't shoot heat beams out of our eyes, leap to the top of a building, outrun bullets, or bend steel beams with our bare hands. At least not yet. But the human—and animal—world is full of some pretty amazing triumphs of flight, sight, speed, and strength. Science, engineering, technology, and a lot of inspiration from nature have allowed humans a little taste of Superman's skills. From fantastic feats of strength to supersonic speed, the impossible becomes possible when we start thinking like super heroes.

FACT:

Superman made his first appearance in *Action Comics* #1 in 1938.

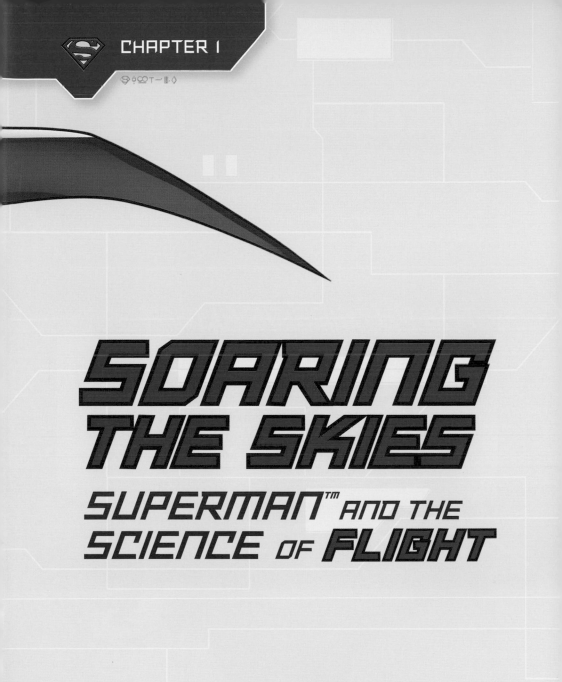

CHAPTER 1

SOARING THE SKIES

SUPERMAN™ AND THE SCIENCE OF FLIGHT

FLIGHT LESSONS

One second Clark Kent peels off his shirt and tie. The next, Superman soars over Metropolis. Flight is child's play for Superman, but it challenged scientists and engineers for centuries. Now their discoveries in flight science allow us to touch the clouds.

THE PHYSICS OF FLIGHT

Flight takes many forms. Birds flap their wings and airplanes use jet engines. But both must deal with gravity. Gravity is the force that pulls all objects toward Earth. Everything dropped, launched, or flown falls to Earth unless it overcomes gravity. To do that, fliers must employ thrust to move them forward through the air. Aircraft get thrust from their powerful engines. Birds experience thrust when they flap their wings.

But forward thrust alone won't keep fliers airborne. They must also create lift, or an upward force, to overcome gravity. Birds and planes have shaped wings to help create lift, but they only work when moving. An airplane doesn't create lift if its engines fail to push it forward. And while birds can glide without flapping, gravity pulls them down as their thrust decreases.

Commercial jets use powerful engines and shaped wings to achieve the thrust and lift necessary for liftoff.

LOW ENERGY LIFT

Eagles and other birds of prey are experts at creating lift with little effort. Their heavy bodies make flapping tiresome. Instead, these birds seek out thermal currents. Without flapping, they ride rising pockets of warm air upward for hundreds of feet.

AERODYNAMIC AIRFOIL

Does Superman's cape hold the secret to his flight powers? No. But the way it cuts through the air might just give the Man of Steel a little extra lift. In the real world, the shape of an airplane's wings is the key to staying airborne.

Otto Lilienthal with one of his gliders in 1895.

The design of the modern airplane wing dates back more than 120 years. In the 1890s bird wings inspired German engineer Otto Lilienthal to experiment with airfoils. An airfoil is a gently curved blade shape that causes air to move quicker over its top than its bottom. This movement creates lower air pressure above the wing to suck it upward. Meanwhile, the angle of the wing redirects air downward. As air is pushed down, the wing experiences lift as it is pushed up.

FLAP

Flaps increase an airfoil's curve to improve lift during takeoffs.

Staying aloft is one thing, but how does an airfoil help a heavy passenger jet take off? At takeoff, pilots lower flaps on the back of a jet's wings. These flaps make the airfoil's curve larger to increase lift. At 160 to 180 miles (258 to 290 kilometers) per hour, enough lift is created to raise the jet. While flying, the flaps are retracted to reduce air resistance, or drag. The reduced drag helps the plane cruise at 550 to 580 miles (885 to 933 km) per hour.

STOPPING POWER

Aircraft wings are shaped to reduce drag, but they also have features to increase it. Why? Because stopping a loaded plane landing at 150 miles (240 km) per hour is no small feat. Jets need more than their brakes to stop. They also use spoilers. These wing flaps flip up to create more drag to help stop the plane.

SPOILER

MICROGRAVITY

Superman doesn't just have the ability to zoom across the sky. He can also stop in mid-air and hover effortlessly. Even jetpacks don't allow us to do this on Earth. But the rules change in space.

An astronaut experiences microgravity.

In space, microgravity rules. Microgravity means very little gravity. In orbit, spacecraft are actually constantly falling toward Earth. In this free-fall microgravity environment, astronauts feel what it's like to be Superman. The lightest push off the wall or floor sends astronauts zooming.

But microgravity comes with some drawbacks. When getting used to microgravity, astronauts may flail about and feel like they're falling. They must hook themselves to footholds to do simple tasks without floating away. A stomach-dropping, roller coaster feeling lasts for days. And even though their eyes tell them they are upside down or sideways, their brains are confused by not feeling gravity's pull. This disorientation often causes vomiting and appetite loss.

KRYPTON

Superman's home planet, Krypton, has a stronger gravitational pull than Earth's. To Superman, Earth must feel like a microgravity environment. In some ways he experiences Earth similar to astronauts on the Moon. The Moon's gravity is only about 17 percent of Earth's. If you weigh 100 pounds (45 kilograms) on Earth, you'll weigh only 17 pounds (8 kg) on the Moon. Because you are "lighter" you can jump six times higher with the same effort.

HUMAN HIGH-FLIERS

Superman is a symbol of our desire to be better, stronger, and faster. Likewise, his ability to soar the skies is a reminder of our long-held fascination with flight. And that fascination has led to some pretty amazing contraptions.

FOUNDERS OF FLIGHT

Dreams of human flight date back hundreds of years. In the 1400s Leonardo DaVinci created more than 100 drawings that showed his ideas for flying machines. But it wasn't until the 1890s that human flight really took off. Otto Lilienthal's attempts to fly the first gliders inspired the scientists and engineers who eventually shaped the future of flight.

Two of those people were Orville and Wilbur Wright. Building on Lilienthal's ideas, the Wright brothers ushered in the era of powered flight. On December 17, 1903, their plane lifted off in Kitty Hawk, North Carolina. It stayed aloft for just 12 seconds and only covered about 120 feet (37 meters). But that short hop changed flight forever.

Orville Wright

Wilbur Wright

Orville Wright flies one of his early planes at Fort Myer, Virginia, in September 1908.

In a few short years, flight innovation skyrocketed. In 1914 planes were used in World War I (1914–1918) spy missions. By the end of the war, they were being used for bombing runs and air combat. Not long after, overseas flight became a reality. On June 14, 1919, John Alcock and Arthur Brown made the first nonstop flight across the Atlantic. It took them 16 hours in a modified British Vimy bomber.

THE FIRST HELICOPTER

Igor Sikorsky developed the rotor designs for the first successful mass-produced helicopter. His skeletal VS-300 took flight on September 14, 1939. It made helicopter history by staying airborne for only a few seconds. But modern helicopters still use Sikorsky's main rotor and tail rotor design today.

UNPOWERED FLIGHT

The Man of Steel flies completely unassisted. He punches through the clouds without jet engines or rocket boosters. Can humans do anything similar?

Human-powered flight has fascinated inventors for decades. And some have even achieved it. In 1979 Bryan Allen piloted the Gossamer Albatross across the English Channel. This 70-pound (32-kg) pedal-powered plane made the 22.5-mile (36-km) flight in 2 hours and 49 minutes. To stay up, Allen pedaled nonstop.

Hang gliders rely on rising pockets of air to stay airborne.

More commonly, people achieve unpowered flight with hang gliders. These triangular airfoils produce lift with a running takeoff from a hill or mountain. The glider then catches ridge and thermal lifts to gain altitude. Ridge lifts occur when air pushes upward as wind hits a cliff. Thermal lifts are rising hot air pockets. Hang gliders can stay aloft for hours at a time, soaring hundreds of miles.

Wingsuiters may come the closest to feeling like Superman in flight. These daredevils jump from planes wearing suits with arm and leg flaps. The flaps catch air to allow wingsuiters to slow down and glide. While a skydiver reaches 120 miles (193 km) per hour in free fall, wingsuiters fall at only 50 to 60 miles (80 to 97 km) per hour. Slight body movements help wingsuiters steer and change direction in mid-flight. They release parachutes for safe landings.

wingsuit

A wingsuiter glides like a super hero high above the ground.

JET PACKS

Unpowered flight can only take humans so far. To really fly like Superman, scientists and engineers have stepped up the game with jet packs.

Military engineers began developing jet packs as early as the 1940s. By 1960 Bell Aerosystems produced the Bell Rocket Belt for the U.S. Army. Fueled by hydrogen peroxide, it could stay aloft for only 21 seconds. Although engineers tried changing it to jet power, the military eventually shelved their jet pack plans.

A Bell Rocket Belt 2 is on display at the National Air and Space Museum's Steven F. Udvar-Hazy Center in Chantilly, Virginia.

Riders race above the waves with water-propelled jet packs.

More recently private tinkerers have taken up the quest for functional jet packs. In the early 2000s, Canadian Raymond Li developed a jet pack propelled by water. His Jetlev-Flyer produces up to 500 pounds (227 kg) of thrust to send riders soaring above the water.

Even more amazing are the flying feats of Swiss pilot Yves "Jetman" Rossy. He is famous for flying like an eagle by strapping on a rigid wing with four tiny jet engines. His 15-minute trips reach speeds of up to 190 miles (306 km) per hour. His wings have taken him over the Alps and across the English Channel.

SPRINGTAIL EFV

Jetman Rossy may soon have to share his jet pack fame. The Springtail Exoskeleton Flying Vehicle (EFV) uses a single engine to power fan blades. This futuristic-looking craft can fly for two hours and reach a top speed of 113 miles (182 km) per hour. It can also hover in place.

SOLAR-POWERED FLIGHT

Superman gets his power from Earth's yellow Sun. The Man of Steel soaks up our Sun's rays to recharge his abilities. But our flying machines need more than the Sun to keep them going, right? Actually, solar-powered aircraft are a reality.

Photovoltaic cells allow solar panels to harness the Sun's power.

The Solar Impulse 2 is powered by the 17,000 photovoltaic cells on its wings. These cells collect sunlight to power its propellers by day and recharge its batteries at night. Although its wingspan is longer than an Airbus A340's, the Solar Impulse 2 weighs only as much as an average car. On July 3, 2015, the aircraft completed an entirely solar-powered flight across the Pacific. It flew from Japan to Hawaii in 118 hours. It set a record for the longest solo flight without refueling.

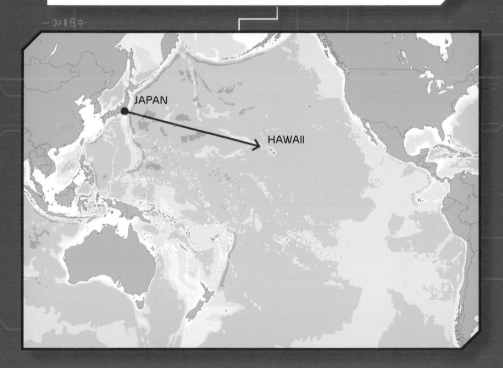

The Solar Impulse 2 isn't the only solar high-flier. The Bristol 2015 Solar Balloon is the first solar hot-air passenger balloon. Bristol is half black to absorb heat from the Sun. Its other half is insulated silver to hold in the heat. The pilot operates vents to spin the balloon, keeping the black part facing the Sun. On August 16, 2015, the solar balloon stayed aloft for 25 minutes on its first flight. It hardly relied on its back-up propane burner.

ALIENS AMONG US

Thrusting his arm skyward, Superman glides between skyscrapers, zooms across the globe, and hovers at will. Obviously he's not bound by our planet's laws of physics. But are there Earth dwellers among us that also appear to defy natural laws? You bet. Some animals perform unbelievable feats of flight.

ECCENTRIC ANIMALS

You'll find birds, bugs, and Superman hanging out in the sky. But fish, squirrels, and snakes stick to water and land, right? Not all of them. Some amazing critters break beyond their natural habitats.

Imagine cruising the ocean only to see a flying fish soar past at 37 miles (60 km) per hour. Forty species of flying fish live in Earth's oceans. Their rapidly beating tails launch them from the sea to avoid predators. Using wing-like fins, they glide 4 feet (1.2 m) above the water for up to 655 feet (200 m) at a time. That's more than the length of two football fields!

flying fish

Not to be outdone by ocean dwellers, a few unlikely land animals also take to the air. Flying squirrels use flaps between their front and back legs to soar up to 150 feet (46 m) from tree to tree. Paradise tree snakes glide for up to 330 feet (101 m) by flexing their bodies to sail through treetops. And Wallace's flying frogs glide through the jungles of Malaysia and Borneo. How? With membranes between their toes and skin flaps on their sides.

flying squirrel

Wallace's flying frog

paradise tree snake

UNBELIEVABLE BIRDS

Flying to the other side of the world is a snap for Superman. In the real world, several bird species make comparable migrations. The Arctic tern travels from Greenland to Antarctica each year. This 44,000-mile (71,000-km) trip zigzags across the Atlantic following favorable wind currents. Over its 30-year life span, the tern flies about 1.5 million miles (2.4 million km). That's like flying to the Moon and back three times.

Arctic tern

sooty terns

The Arctic tern flies far, but the tropical sooty tern flies long. It stays airborne from the time it leaves the nest until it returns to lay eggs. Just how long is that? Up to five years! In flight, the sooty tern swoops down to pluck fish from water or to snatch up flying fish. And its shrill call sounds like "wide-a-wake." That's an apt call, since they sleep only a couple of seconds at a time in flight.

HUMMINGBIRD ACROBATICS

The ruby-throated hummingbird can't walk and can barely hop with its tiny legs. But it beats its wings 53 times each second to hover and fly upside down and backward. It also eats twice its weight in food each day to have enough energy to accomplish these feats.

AMAZING ARTHROPODS

Superman's flight powers are unexplainable. How does he take off unassisted? What keeps him in the air? Sometimes insect flight is equally mystifying.

Insect flight doesn't always follow the same rules as bird and plane flight. Tiny bumblebee wings don't look like airfoils. And they hardly look large enough to keep the husky bees aloft. But by fluttering incredibly fast, bumblebee wings create tiny vortexes. These low-pressure areas above the wings generate lift to keep the bee flying.

bumblebee

FACT:

The painted lady butterfly makes a 4,000-mile (6,437-km) migration from North Africa to Iceland.

blowfly

The blowfly's flight is only understandable with the aid of high-powered X-ray technology. With this technology scientists discovered the fly uses muscles smaller than human hair to beat its wings 150 times per second. These muscles are not attached directly to its wings. Instead they are inside the fly's thorax. As the fly changes the shape of its thorax, the movements are transferred to the wings.

ROBOBEE

Harvard scientists applied their knowledge of a fly's biology to create RoboBee. This tiny robot flaps its paper-thin wings 120 times per second. Future jobs for RoboBee could include crop pollination and search and rescue missions.

SOARING SEEDS

The Man of Steel doesn't strap on an engine. He doesn't slip into a set of wings. He just gently lifts into the air and glides for miles. This simple, graceful flight dance can be seen in nature nowhere better than with seed dispersion.

The maple seed uses a helicopter shape to travel to new planting grounds.

Seeds come in a variety of amazing shapes—including some that look like helicopters, gliders, and parachutes. Helicopter maple seeds use the same aerodynamic trick as insects and hummingbirds. They create a tornado-like vortex. By spinning, the seedpods lift upward with more than twice the gravity-fighting power of non-swirling seeds.

Indonesian Javan cucumber seeds, at 6 inches (15 cm) across, are among the largest of any winged seeds. Unlike spinning seeds, these gliding seedpods are incredibly thin. They sail along on wind currents, finding resting places far from their parent plant. To survive, the seedlings must grow where their vines don't have to compete for soil and water.

The dandelion plant propels its seeds with tiny tufted parachutes. Breezes as gentle as 4 miles (6.4 km) per hour can carry the seeds up to 330 feet (100 m).

Light-as-air dandelion seeds float on the wind.

WONDERS IN MODERN FLIGHT

Seeing the Man of Steel in flight naturally inspires us to want to fly higher and faster. But flight inventions have already achieved some amazing feats—and they're poised to go even higher.

INNOVATION IN FLIGHT

One secret to Superman's success is his ability to outsmart super-villains. Likewise, some of our greatest innovations in flight come from our need to outthink our enemies. It's no wonder the military is such a hotbed for flight innovation.

Spy and stealth planes are military specialties. The SR-71 Blackbird spy plane was one of the fastest planes ever built. It could fly more than 2,000 miles (3,219 km) per hour. That's three times faster than the speed of sound.

SR-71 Blackbird

Speed is good for making fast getaways. But what about sneaking up on an enemy? That's when you'll need the B-2 Spirit bomber. This 172-foot (52-m) wide boomerang-shaped bomber is virtually undetectable. Its shape, color, and muffled engines keep it hidden in plain sight. More importantly, its composite skin and radar-absorbing paint make it look like an insect on radar scanners.

B-2 Spirit

JUMP JETS

Normal fighter jets need long runways for takeoffs and landings. But not the Harrier Jump Jet. It can take off like a helicopter and fly like a jet. Its revolving jet nozzles give it thrust to lift off short runways and small aircraft carriers. Harriers reach speeds of up to 730 miles (1,175 km) per hour in flight.

CARGO CARRYING

Between his strength and his ability to fly, Superman makes his job look easy. After all, he can guide crashing passenger jets to the ground without breaking much of a sweat. In the real world, however, lifting cargo takes a huge effort—and a huge plane.

The largest cargo carrier in the world is the Russian Antonov An-225. From front to back and wing tip to wing tip, this beast is nearly the size of a football field. It can carry more than 500,000 pounds (226,800 kg), or the weight of about 50 elephants. It hauls anything up to 33 feet (10 m) in diameter and 230 feet (70 m) long. Loads that can't fit inside it can be carried on the An-225's back. All loaded up, it can still fly 500 miles (800 km) per hour.

The nose of the An-225 flips up so large cargo can be easily loaded.

Super Guppy

NASA's Super Guppy is another huge cargo carrier. The Guppy looks more like a fish than a plane. Its hinged nose opens to reveal a large cargo bay. It can carry more than 50,000 pounds (23,680 kg) of cargo. Since 1962, this monster has played a vital role in the transportation of spacecraft parts.

TRANSPORT HELICOPTERS

Planes aren't the only heavy lifters. The Mi26 transport helicopter can easily hoist and carry a 737 jetliner. This massive chopper uses an eight-blade propeller. It can carry 20-ton (18-metric ton) loads at 183 miles (295 km) per hour.

DRONES

When super-villains strike, the citizens of Metropolis can count on Superman to swoop in and save the day. In our world we've discovered ways to sit back and let high-fliers handle our toughest jobs. More unmanned aerial vehicles (UAVs) fly our skies today than at any other time in history.

Military UAVs are invaluable in sticky situations. Piloted by a crew miles away, Reaper and Predator drones scout sites ahead of troops or manned vehicles. Pilots use onboard cameras to guide their flights. In the dark, infrared cameras give them night vision. Reapers and Predators help troops in battle by locating and destroying specific targets.

A Predator drone is controlled remotely by a pilot on the ground.

Recreational drones have built-in digital cameras to provide an eye in the sky.

Although military drones have been at work for years, drone use by regular people is rising quickly. Some experts think more than 30,000 drones will be flying overhead in the U.S. alone by 2020. Many owners use their personal drones for making movies and taking photos. And companies are gearing up for drone use too. Agricultural companies have developed drones to help farmers scout crop conditions on large farms. Real estate agents use drones to film virtual tours of houses for sale. One company in England has even tested out drones for pizza delivery.

THE FIRST UAV

UAVs have been around since the 1860s. Charles Perley's aerial bomber was used in the American Civil War (1861–1865). This UAV was a hot-air balloon loaded with explosives and a timing mechanism.

INCREDIBLE SPACECRAFT

Superman can fly well beyond the upper reaches of the clouds. Whether guiding a nuclear warhead into space or flying to an alien planet, nothing holds him back. For humans, space flight was only a long-held dream for thousands of years. But now science and engineering give us the power to achieve those dreams.

For more than 50 years, rockets have been our ticket off Earth. They have delivered people to the Moon, robots to Mars, and probes to the very edges of our solar system. While they come in many shapes and sizes, they all work in similar ways. Rockets burn fuel to produce hot gases. These gases expand and blast downward to generate incredible thrust. To escape Earth's gravity, a rocket must reach a speed of 25,000 miles (40,230 km) per hour.

Hot gases burst from the bottom of a rocket to thrust it skyward.

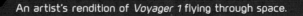

An artist's rendition of *Voyager 1* flying through space.

Traveling beyond our solar system is the next space hurdle. But that quest has already begun. In 1977 NASA launched the *Voyager 1* space probe. In 2012 it achieved interstellar flight when it reached the edge of our solar system. At its current speed, it would reach our nearest neighboring star in 40,000 years. Unfortunately *Voyager 1* is expected to run out of fuel around 2025, long before it ever gets there.

MANEUVERS

Superman can pull off some pretty fancy flight maneuvers. For him, performing mid-flight turns, spins, and hovers are a piece of cake. In the real world, it takes specially trained pilots to perform tricky maneuvers.

An aerobatic pilot heads into a roll.

Rolls, spins, and loops are some of the basic maneuvers used by fighter jet and stunt pilots. In a roll, a pilot spins the plane on its longitudinal axis. This imaginary line passes through the aircraft from its nose to its tail. In a spin, the plane plummets downward in a spiral. A pilot pulls up the nose of the plane to head backward into a loop. While these maneuvers appear effortless, the pilot must carefully calculate speed and direction. Pilots rely on their instruments when they lose sight of the horizon. When pilots can't see land, they often lose the ability to know if they are flying upright.

Another danger to stunt pilots is the strain to their bodies from the g-forces. Standing still we feel one 'g' from the force of gravity. But flight maneuvers strain pilots' bodies with forces larger than gravity. A force twice that of gravity is 2 g's. A force three times greater than gravity is 3 g's and so on. Pilots experience 3 to 4 g's in a loop maneuver. These g-forces pull the blood away from pilots' brains and into lower parts of their bodies. This blood loss could cause untrained pilots to lose vision or pass out. Military pilots wear g-suits to squeeze blood back up to their brains.

POURING WATER UP

Airplane maneuvers can really mess with physics. Stunt pilots can pour water up when flying upside down. This is possible if the plane is accelerating downward faster than gravity's pull. The water appears to be moving up when, in fact, it is falling downward. It's just dropping slower than the plane.

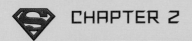

CHAPTER 2

SEEING THROUGH WALLS

SUPERMAN™ AND THE SCIENCE OF SIGHT

HUMAN SIGHT

The first time the people of Metropolis saw a blue blur zipping across the sky, they were stunned to see a man in flight. But they may not have stopped to think about something equally as amazing: their ability to see Superman in the first place. Take a peek at the science that makes sight possible.

LIGHT AND SIGHT

Understanding the science of sight begins with light. Just like Superman did as a baby, sunlight travels through space to reach our planet. But it doesn't travel on a rocket ship. It travels in energy waves. The full range of energy waves from the Sun is called the electromagnetic spectrum.

THE ELECTROMAGNETIC SPECTRUM

Radio waves | Micro-waves | Infrared radiation | Visible light | Ultraviolet | X-rays | Gamma-rays

Electromagnetic waves can be long, short, or somewhere in between. Most of these waves are invisible. We can't see shorter, higher energy waves such as gamma rays, X-rays, and ultraviolet light. We also can't see longer, lower energy infrared light waves, microwaves, and radio waves. Visible light, which is in the middle of the spectrum, is the only light energy we can see.

We call visible light from the Sun white light. But it's not just one color. It is actually made up of different colors mixed together. The different colors in white light each have a different energy level. Have you learned the name "Roy G. Biv" to remember the colors of the rainbow? It stands for red, orange, yellow, green, blue, indigo, and violet. These colors are always in the same order because they are organized by their energy level. Red light has lower energy than green light. And violet light has the highest energy of all visible light.

A prism is a piece of glass that can split white light into the colors of the rainbow.

HUMAN VISION

Vision depends on your eyes' ability to detect light energy. How do they do it? Reflected light and the parts of your eyes are the keys.

Light reflects off everything around you. When you look at something, such as a tree, you see it because light bounces off it and into your eye. This light passes through your pupil and lens. It then makes an upside down and backward image of the tree on the retina at the back of the eye.

Upside down and backward images are projected onto the back of the eye.

The retina has cells called rods and cones that are sensitive to light. Rods are most sensitive to light and dark changes. They help you see at low light levels. Cones are active at higher light levels. They allow you to see color. The rods and cones change the image into an electrical signal. That signal zips through the optic nerve and directly to your brain. Your brain tells you what you see.

PARTS OF THE HUMAN EYE

IRIS
uses a ring of
muscle fibers to
open and close
the pupil

PUPIL
changes size
to let more or
less light into
the eye

CORNEA
bends light into the
eye and protects
the eye from wind
and dust

OPTIC NERVE
carries messages
from the retina to
the brain

RETINA
contains light-sensitive
rods and cones, which
change light into an
electrical signal that the
brain understands

LENS
changes shape
to focus light
onto the retina

SEEING COLOR

Superman's eyes can see through walls and shoot beams to cut through steel. Although we can only wish for these powers, our eyes do have the amazing ability to see a remarkable range of colors. In fact most people can see about one million colors. How? It's a tag-team combo of reflected light and the cones in our eyes.

The color of an object depends on the wavelengths of light it reflects and absorbs. For instance, a ripe banana looks yellow because it absorbs every color wavelength except yellow. The yellow wavelengths are reflected. Likewise, an apple looks red because it absorbs every color wavelength except red.

But reflecting and absorbing colors is only half of the story. Each of your eyes has about six million cone cells in its retina. And each one of those cones is most sensitive to red, green, or blue. When you see a banana, the reflected light stimulates the cones in the retina to different degrees. A signal then travels along the optic nerve to your brain. Your brain processes the signal and tells you that you're seeing yellow.

CONES AND RODS OF THE RETINA

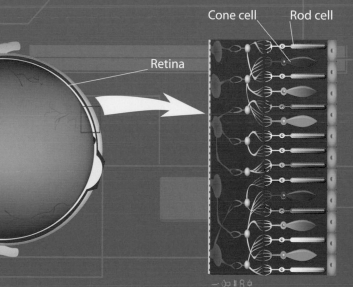

Cone cell

Rod cell

Retina

COLOR BLINDNESS

Some people have cone cells that lack certain color-sensitive pigments. This condition causes color blindness. About 1 in 12 men and 1 in 200 women are red-green color blind. That means they can't easily tell the difference between red and green. In very rare cases, people can also be blue-yellow color blind. And absolutely color-blind people are the most rare. They only see the world in shades of gray.

ENHANCING SIGHT

Clark Kent may wear glasses, but he certainly doesn't need them to see. They are part of his clever disguise as a mild-mannered reporter. For the rest of us, glasses, as well as microscopes and telescopes, actually improve our vision.

CORRECTIVE LENSES

People need glasses when the lenses in their eyes don't curve correctly to focus clearly on an object. For some people, an incorrect curve causes nearsightedness. They can see things up close, but objects in the distance look blurry. For others, a different incorrect curve causes farsightedness. They can see faraway objects, but close ones are blurry.

CONCAVE LENS

Glasses have custom-made lenses that bend light to help focus it on the retina. Concave lenses help nearsighted people see faraway objects. These lenses are thinner in the middle than around the edges. Light passing through these lenses bends outward.

Farsighted people use convex lenses to help them see up-close objects. Convex lenses are thin at the edges but thick in the middle. They bend light inward.

CONVEX
LENS

LASER SURGERY

Glasses aren't the only option for correcting vision. For a more permanent solution, some people choose laser eye surgery. Surgeons use lasers to carefully reshape and correct the corneas. Once they're repaired, no additional lenses are needed in front of the eyes to correct vision.

MICROSCOPES

Superman can see at the microscopic level, and we can too! But because we weren't born on Krypton, we need microscopes to do it. Visit any lab in the world and you'll likely find a compound microscope. Like eyeglasses, these microscopes use lenses to bend light. Instead of just bringing objects into focus, these lenses make objects look hundreds of times larger.

Binocular compound microscopes have two eyepieces instead of one.

Compound microscopes magnify objects by using at least two lenses. The lens closest to your eye is called the eyepiece. The lens nearest the object you are looking at is called the objective lens. The objective lens magnifies an object first. Then the eyepiece magnifies the image from the objective lens a second time.

Microscopes allow us to explore a world that is normally too small to see. Scientists use them to study plant cells, insect wings, and other tiny living and nonliving things. Doctors use microscopes to study blood and tissue samples. And companies that create tiny objects—such as computer chips—use microscopes to inspect their products.

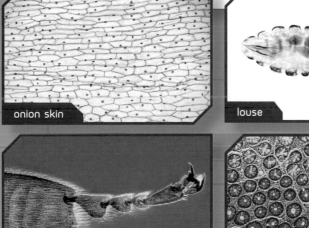

onion skin

louse

bee leg

human tissue

ELECTRON MICROSCOPES

Electron microscopes are the most powerful microscopes on the planet. Instead of rays of light, they use beams of electrons to create a very detailed image of the tiniest things. While compound microscopes magnify objects up to about 2,000 times, electron microscopes can magnify objects a million times or more! They allowed scientists to see viruses and atoms for the first time. And they can show everyday items—such as pollen grains or an ant's head—in amazing detail.

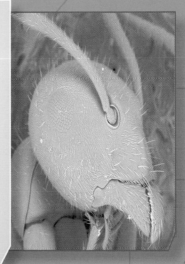

TELESCOPES

Superman has the eyes of a hawk. He can focus his sight to see objects clearly from miles away. For mere mortals like ourselves, the tool we use to see great distances is a telescope. Most telescopes are either refracting or reflecting telescopes.

Like microscopes, refracting telescopes use an objective lens and an eyepiece. But instead of making small objects look bigger, these lenses make distant objects look closer. To do this, the objective lens collects light from a distant object. Then the eyepiece magnifies it to make it look closer. The bigger the objective lens, the brighter the image and the more it can be magnified.

Lens

Eyepiece

Incoming Light

Image

Incoming Light

Refracting telescopes use a large lens to direct the light into the eyepiece.

FACT:

Binoculars are just two small telescopes attached to each other, one for each eye.

Eyepiece

Incoming Light

Primary Mirror

Secondary
Mirror

Image

Incoming Light

Reflecting telescopes use mirrors
to bounce light into the eyepiece.

Reflecting telescopes work similarly to refracting
telescopes. But instead of an objective lens, they use a
primary mirror to gather light. This curved mirror reflects
the light toward the secondary mirror. This mirror then
reflects the light to the eyepiece. The eyepiece magnifies
the object to make it look closer.

GREAT CANARY TELESCOPE

The Great Canary Telescope is the
world's largest telescope and, like
most big telescopes, a reflector.
It sits on a mountaintop in the
Canary Islands off the northwest
coast of Africa. Its mirror spans
34.1 feet (10.4 m) across.

SPACE TELESCOPES

If Superman needs to peer deep into space, he flies above Earth's atmosphere. Why? Because it's a lot easier to see the universe without Earth's hazy atmosphere getting in the way. Not surprisingly, the same holds true for telescopes. The best telescopes for studying the stars are not on Earth at all. They're circling it in space.

This image, called "eXtreme Deep Field," is a combination of exposures taken over a 10-year period. At its highest resolution, it shows about 5,500 galaxies.

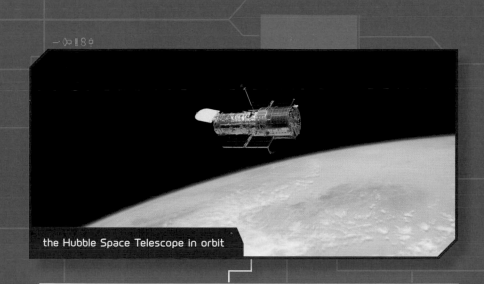

the Hubble Space Telescope in orbit

The Hubble Space Telescope is the most famous off-world spyglass. This reflecting telescope was launched in 1990 and is as big as a school bus. Its nearly 8-foot- (2. 4-m-) wide mirror gathers and focuses light at a digital sensor. This sensor can collect and combine images over hundreds of hours. When the light hits the sensor for that long, the telescope captures images of objects billions of light years away. Hubble has provided scientists with the clearest views of planets, stars, nebulas, and galaxies in the history of space exploration.

SPITZER SPACE TELESCOPE

Not all space telescopes see light the same way. The Spitzer Space Telescope (STT), gathers infrared light, which carries heat. Using the STT, scientists detect objects that are too faint to be observed by visible light, such as very distant planets, stars, and nebulas. The STT has been helping scientists explore the universe since 2003. It is the size of a car and houses a 33.5-inch- (85-cm-) wide mirror.

ANIMAL VISION

Considering Superman is an alien from another planet, it's not totally surprising that his vision is so different from ours. What may be surprising is the number of creatures on Earth whose eyes seem just as alien as his!

NO EYES, MANY EYES

When it comes to animal sight, eyeballs aren't the only option. Many animals have compound eyes. These eyes are made up of hundreds of separate units. The more units, the better the animal can see. An ant's eye has several hundred units. A housefly has a few thousand. And dragonflies can have 30,000 units in each eye. Compound eyes are excellent at detecting motion. That's one of the reasons it can be difficult to swat a fly. It spots your hand moving toward it. But compound eyes aren't so good at seeing fine details.

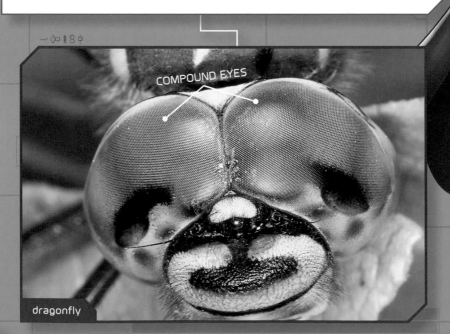

COMPOUND EYES

dragonfly

Other animals don't have eyes in the traditional sense at all. Earthworms have hundreds of little light-sensitive cells called eyespots around their heads and tails. These cells help them find the cool, dark places they like to go. Leeches, caterpillars, and jellyfish have eyespots too. And sea stars can have an eyespot on each arm. Depending on the species, a sea star can have up to 40 eyes! But even with all those eyes, they don't see much. They mostly detect the direction of light and large shadows.

BELL

A jellyfish has tiny eyespots located around its bell.

SCALLOPS

Scallops probably win as the most-eyed creatures on Earth. A single scallop may have more than 100 eyes! Each of these eyes, located all around its mantle, has a lens and retina. They work together to alert the animal of changes in light and motion. The scallop can see very rough images—enough to warn it against predators.

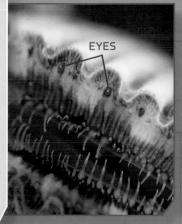

EYES

EAGLE-EYED

Although our eyesight isn't as sharp as Superman's, some animals have incredibly keen peepers. The term "eagle-eyed" exists for good reason—eagles have very sharp eyesight! They can see four to five times farther than the average person. If you swapped eyes with an eagle, you could stand on top of a 10-story building and see an ant crawling on the ground. You could even spot a rabbit from more than 1 mile (1.6 km) away. Now that's super hero-level eyesight!

Bald eagles use their keen eyesight to swoop down and snatch fish right out of the water.

Eagles see so well because their eyes are huge. Although the average eagle only weighs about 10 pounds (4.5 kg), its eyes can be as large as an adult human's. Bigger eyes mean better vision because they let in more light. And the larger the eye, the larger the image projected onto the retina.

Larger eyes see finer details, much like a large TV screen shows more details than a small tablet screen.

Imagine watching a movie on a tablet versus a big-screen TV. You can see many more details on the larger screen. Eagle retinas are also more densely coated with cones than ours. They allow the birds to see much more clearly than we do. In addition eagles have excellent color vision and can see ultraviolet light too.

NIGHT VISION

The power to see through the darkest night isn't just for super heroes. Some animals have night vision too. Nocturnal animals are most active at night. To help them see, their huge eyes have wider pupils, larger lenses, and larger retinas. These features allow their eyes to collect more light in dark conditions. For example, owls have eyes that fill more than one half of their skulls. Their forward-facing eyes are so big they can't move them. To make up for their fixed eyes, they can swivel their heads 270 degrees. This ability gives them a wide field of view.

Owls use their huge eyes to hunt at night.

The *tapetum lucidum* in a shark's eye glows when it reflects light.

Some animals have reflectors, called the *tapetum lucidum*, in the backs of their eyes. These reflectors can double the amount of light their eyes can use. Have you ever seen a cat at night with glowing eyes? What you're seeing is the tapetum reflecting light. Other animals with tapetums include raccoons, cows, sharks, crocodiles, deer, zebras, lions, and moths.

FIELD OF VIEW

How much an animal can see without turning its head is called its field of view. Predators, such as lions, wolves, and owls, have eyes that face forward. Their eyes give them good depth perception, which helps them find and catch prey. Prey animals, such as deer, zebras, and chickens, have eyes that face sideways. Their depth perception is not too good. But their side-facing eyes give them a large field of vision. They can see almost all the way around their bodies, usually giving them time to see and flee predators.

SEEING THE UNSEEN

Eagles aren't alone among animals with the amazing ability to see invisible light. Bees use ultraviolet (UV) vision to see special patterns on flower petals, which help guide them to the nectar. Other insects, such as butterflies, use their UV vision to help find mates and food. Once thought to be rare among mammals, at least 40 different species also sense UV light. Cats, dogs, ferrets, and hedgehogs all see UV. Even reindeer can see some UV light. It helps them find food and avoid predators in harsh Arctic conditions.

Bees and butterflies use their UV vision powers to find nectar.

Superman is famous for his heat vision. He can use it to melt obstacles in his way. Remarkably, some animals have "heat vision" too. But instead of melting things, they sense infrared light, which gives off heat, to understand the world around them. For example, boas and pythons have pits lined with heat sensors along their jaws. Pit vipers have a sensor-lined membrane stretched above a pit between their eyes and nose. Vampire bats can also sense heat given off by their prey by using pits around their noses. And some beetles have heat-sensing organs on their legs or beneath their wings.

Through heat sensors, royal boas detect infrared light given off by prey.

BEYOND ORDINARY SIGHT

It's no secret that Superman can melt icebergs using heat vision and see through concrete walls using X-ray vision. But did you know humans also have their own versions of heat and X-ray vision? Check out what we can see with a little help from technology.

HEAT VISION

While Superman, cats, and owls have no problem seeing in dimly lit areas, people need a little help. Luckily, technology can bring things to light. Heat vision, or thermal imaging, is one way to do it.

Thermal imaging equipment detects infrared light waves. These invisible waves carry heat. All objects give off some amount of infrared waves. Thermal cameras change these invisible waves into light you can see. They can detect people, animals, and objects by the heat patterns they emit.

40.3 °C

20.3

Thermal cameras detect heat given off by everything, including us.

A firefighter uses a thermal camera to pick up heat signatures in a house.

Thermal imaging can be used at night for seeing in the dark. It is also used during the day to see things through smoke, heavy fog, and dust storms. Firefighters use thermal imaging to help find people in smoke-filled buildings. Thermal imaging equipment is also used by the military and police for security purposes. It can reveal whether an area has been recently disturbed, such as when something is buried in the ground. Law enforcement has used thermal imaging to find hidden drugs, money, and bodies.

SEEING GREEN

Using heat isn't the only way to see in low-light conditions. Image enhancement is another technology that people use to see in the dark. Image enhancement gives us the eerie, glowing green night-vision images people see on TV and in the movies.

54° 25' 30" N - 18° 39' 15" E

Night-vision goggles make it possible for humans to use infrared light.

Image enhancement equipment gathers any available light and makes the most of it. Even in the dimmest conditions, there is some light present. Some of this light may be infrared light that we can't see with our eyes. Night-vision equipment that uses image enhancement technology boosts every tiny bit of light available, including the infrared, so you can see in the dark.

So why do night-vision goggles with image enhancement show green images? Because enhancing the light causes some details and all colors to be lost. To make up for the lost colors, the goggles make everything green. Why not blue, red, or yellow? Because human eyes are more sensitive to green than any other color.

X-RAY VISION

When it comes to his eyes, Superman's most famous power is his X-ray vision. In comic books and movies, this superpower allows him to peer through walls as if they were invisible. In real life, X-rays work a little differently.

X-rays are a high-energy form of electromagnetic radiation that we can't see. These rays have so much energy they can travel through things that ordinary, visible light can't. X-rays are often used in medicine to diagnose and treat illnesses.

X-rays show us the bones hidden beneath our skin.

Medical X-rays are made by placing the part of the body to be examined between a beam of X-rays and a plate containing film. Hard materials like bones absorb X-rays very well. Soft tissues, such as skin and muscle, allow the rays to pass right through. The X-rays that pass through the body strike the photographic plate. Dense bones show up as white and softer tissues look gray.

FACT:

The ability of X-rays to damage living tissue can be used for good. X-rays are used to kill cancer cells in radiation therapy treatment.

A nurse wears a lead-lined apron while working with a patient in an X-ray room.

As X-rays pass through the body, they can damage living tissue because they are so energetic. For this reason lead-lined aprons are often placed over body parts we don't want X-rays to pass through. Lead blocks X-rays because it is so dense. Interestingly, lead is the one material Superman's X-ray vision can't see through either.

WILHELM ROENTGEN

German physicist Wilhelm Roentgen discovered X-rays in 1895. He called them "X" rays because he didn't know what they were. The very first image taken using X-rays was of his wife's hand. When she saw the picture of the bones beneath her skin, she exclaimed, "I have seen my death." Roentgen won the first Nobel Prize in Physics in 1901 for his discovery.

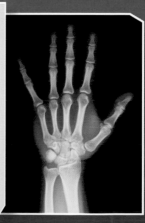

X-RAY USES

X-rays aren't just used for medicine. For decades they've been used in airport security to check bags for dangerous items. X-rays pass right through soft leather, plastic, and fabric. They are blocked by metal and can reveal guns, knives, and other weapons hidden in luggage.

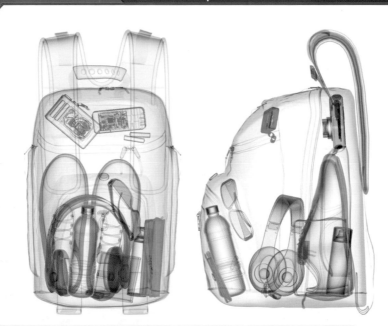

Invented for medical purposes, X-ray technology now has many uses.

X-rays have many other uses, including checking for cracks and fatigue in metal parts in machines, such as jet engines. They are also used in the art world to help determine if a painting is a fake. X-rays can uncover the types of minerals used in the paint and pinpoint where the painting was made. X-rays can also reveal earlier versions or completely different images under the layers of paint. These clues can help determine if a painting was really created by a famous artist.

X-rays can even be used to examine mummies without unwrapping them. The mummy of Tutankhamen, or King Tut, was scanned with X-rays as a type of "virtual autopsy." The scans showed he had a variety of health issues. These issues included a badly broken leg, which probably led to his death.

SEEING THROUGH WALLS

Superman uses his X-ray vision to spot villains lurking behind walls. Researchers at the Massachusetts Institute of Technology have also come up with a system that can "see" through walls. This technology, called "Wi-Vi," sends out a low-power WiFi signal. It pings out radio waves and then tracks how they're bounced back. Since radio waves can pass through solid objects, they can track people moving in closed rooms or behind walls.

THE FUTURE OF SIGHT

Superman-like sight may be in our future. Scientists and engineers are developing all sorts of exciting technologies to enhance our vision. In fact a telescopic contact lens has already been invented. It allows people to zoom in their vision almost three times. It was created to help people with age-related macular degeneration (AMD). This condition makes it difficult to see fine details, such as type on a page. Telescopic contacts allow people with AMD to zoom in on these details.

A woman takes an eye test to detect AMD.

Researchers at the University of Michigan have also developed a super-thin infrared light sensor that could be layered onto contact lenses. This sensor could one day be used to allow people to see in the dark. Instead of wearing bulky night-vision goggles, soldiers would simply pop in a pair of contacts.

High-tech contact lenses and bionic eyes
may be the future of superhuman sight.

A bionic eye has also been developed for the legally blind. The Argus II Retinal Prosthesis System uses a tiny camera in a patient's glasses to capture images. The images change into electrical pulses that are sent to an implant in the retina. The implant sends the pulses through the optic nerve to the brain. The brain makes sense of the images and creates patterns of light. Although the Argus II doesn't restore normal vision, it does allow people to sense objects and even see some color.

OUTRUNNING BULLETS

SUPERMAN™ AND THE SCIENCE OF SPEED

WHAT IS SPEED?

For heroes like Superman, speed is essential to staying one step ahead of criminals. In the scientific world, there's more to speed than getting somewhere in a hurry. But what, exactly, is speed, and how does it affect us every day?

SPEED ESSENTIALS

To scientists, speed is how fast an object is moving. It is a measure of the distance traveled in a certain time. Although speed is often associated with "fastness," any moving object has speed. A tortoise inching along has speed, just not as much as a rocket blasting into space.

While defining speed is simple, perceiving it isn't always straightforward. Superman is famous for traveling faster than a speeding bullet, which is about 1,700 miles (2,735 km) per hour. But right now—even standing still—you are traveling faster.

A person standing near Earth's equator spins about 1,040 miles (1,670 km) per hour around Earth's axis. At the same time, Earth whips around the Sun at 67,000 miles (107,800 km) per hour. That's not all. Our solar system hurtles around the center of the Milky Way galaxy at about 490,000 miles (788,580 km) per hour. Now that's fast!

Earth orbits the Sun at the breakneck speed of 67,000 miles (107,800 km) per hour.

STOPPING A BULLET

A speeding bullet only packs a punch when it makes an impact. To stop bullets in the real world, soldiers and police officers use Kevlar. This fabric's strong, light weave stretches to rob bullets of their energy. Kevlar is the life-saving material used in bulletproof vests.

POLICE

ACCELERATION

Superman can go from standing still to a blue blur in the blink of an eye. This awesome ability to speed up is called acceleration. Acceleration is the change in the velocity of a moving object. Imagine riding in a car on a highway. As long as the car maintains a constant speed, you don't feel like you are moving. But if the car suddenly speeds up, brakes, or turns a corner, you feel it. That's acceleration.

Roller coaster riders feel acceleration as they zoom down a hill.

One of the best places to feel acceleration at work is an amusement park. The thrill of roller coasters is in their rapid accelerations. The stomach-dropping feeling you get when a roller coaster plummets down a hill comes from acceleration. As you rapidly speed up, you feel the acceleration. When you squash your buddy while rounding a curve, you feel acceleration because your body changes direction. Even the sudden stop at the end of the ride is a form of acceleration called deceleration.

THE WORLD'S FASTEST ROLLER COASTER

Ferrari World in the United Arab Emirates is home to the world's fastest roller coaster. Formula Rossa maxes out at 149 miles (240 km) per hour. This speedy coaster accelerates from zero to 62 miles (100 km) per hour in just two seconds.

ULTIMATE SPEED

In the super hero world, you'd do well to round out your track team with Superman and The Flash. No one is faster than these two. In our world, you'd definitely want sound and light on your team. Check out the amazing speeds of these two forms of energy.

SPEED OF SOUND

Sometimes Superman flies so fast he becomes supersonic! Supersonic means faster than the speed of sound. Sound is a wave of vibrations that passes through air particles. Starting at a source, vibrations pass from particle to particle until they reach your ear. These vibrations move through the air at the incredible speed of 761 miles (1,225 km) per hour. That's like running the length of almost four football fields in one second.

While sound travels fast, its speed is not beyond human reach. Traveling at or beyond the speed of sound is measured in Mach numbers. A vehicle that reaches Mach 1 is traveling at the speed of sound. At Mach 2, it travels twice the speed of sound. At Mach 3, three times, and so on.

The Bell X-1 was the first aircraft to break the speed of sound. On October 14, 1947, Bell X-1 launched from the bomb bay of a Boeing B-29. It then used a rocket engine to go supersonic. Today most military fighter jets reach speeds of Mach 2 to Mach 3.

Bell X-1

FACT:

On October 15, 1997, the rocket car Thrust SSC became the first car to break the speed of sound. It topped 763 miles (1,228 km) per hour.

SONIC BOOMS

One big drawback to supersonic flight is the sonic boom caused when jets pass the speed of sound. A sonic boom is a loud rumble caused when air molecules are rapidly pushed aside. It is heard and felt by people on the ground when a supersonic plane flies overhead. It can be loud enough to damage people's eardrums and break windows. As a result, supersonic flight is banned over many countries.

An F-18 Super Hornet creates a vapor cone as it nears the speed of sound.

an artist's rendition of NASA's X-43A hypersonic jet in flight

While engineers study ways to reduce sonic booms, the race is on to develop hypersonic planes that fly even faster. To be called hypersonic, an aircraft must reach Mach 5. On November 16, 2004, NASA's X-43A hypersonic jet set the world record as the fastest aircraft. The unmanned aircraft clocked a speed of nearly 7,000 miles (11,265 km) per hour. That's Mach 9.6!

BOOM!

SUPERSONIC PERSON

Can a human reach supersonic speeds without an aircraft? Felix Baumgartner did it. Wearing an astronaut suit, he jumped from a helium balloon 24 miles (39 km) above New Mexico on October 14, 2012. On his way down, he broke the sound barrier, causing a sonic boom, before deploying his parachute. His maximum speed was 834 miles (1,340 km) per hour.

SPEED OF LIGHT

If the speed of sound is incredible, the speed of light is mind-blowing. Light travels at 186,000 miles (300,000 km) per second. At this speed it could circle the Earth's equator seven and a half times in just one second.

In fact, the speed of light is so fast we use it to measure huge distances in space. One light year is the distance a light beam can travel in one year. How far is that? About 6 trillion miles (9 trillion km)! If you think the Moon and Sun are really far away, think again. The Moon is only about 1.3 light seconds from Earth. The Sun is about 8.3 light minutes away.

1.3 LIGHT SECONDS AWAY

8.3 LIGHT MINUTES AWAY

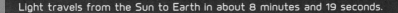

Light travels from the Sun to Earth in about 8 minutes and 19 seconds.

The next nearest star to Earth, Proxima Centuri, is 4.24 light years away. When we see Proxima Centuri, we don't see it as it looks now. We see it as it looked more than four years ago. High-powered telescopes, such as the Hubble Space Telescope, help us see stars millions of light years away. But Hubble actually looks back in time. It sees stars as they looked millions of years ago. Some have burned out before we even discover them.

The Hubble Space Telescope orbits high above Earth's atmosphere, allowing it to see deep into space.

JUNO SPACECRAFT

No human invention has come close to achieving light speed. But NASA's *Juno* spacecraft, launched in 2011, will soon become the fastest human invention. When it orbits Jupiter in 2016, its speed will be about 46 miles (74 km) per second. That's fast, but still just 1/4,000th the speed of light.

ENEMIES OF SPEED

Just as Superman battles the super-villains of Metropolis, speed has some enemies of its own to overcome. Gravity and friction slow things down.

GRAVITY

What goes up, including Superman, must come down. Gravity is the force that pulls everything toward Earth. You see gravity in action when you throw a ball. No matter how high or fast you throw, eventually the ball returns to the ground.

If gravity's pull is so strong, how do planes and rockets overcome it? An airplane's wings create lift to fight gravity. The shape and angle of the wing deflects air downward, creating a push that lifts the plane upward. The faster an airplane travels, the more lift it creates.

Rockets create thrust to combat gravity. To break away from Earth's atmosphere, a rocket must attain a thrust of 25,000 miles (40,230 km) per hour. Massive amounts of burning fuel spew gases that push off Earth to thrust the rocket into space.

An Atlas V rocket uses the downward thrust of gases to launch toward space.

MICROGRAVITY

As the *International Space Station* circles Earth, it's constantly falling toward the planet. So why doesn't it hit the ground? Because its speed of 17,500 miles (28,000 km) per hour matches Earth's curve. Inside the station, astronauts feel very little gravity because they are in constant free fall.

FRICTION

Friction's force always opposes motion. Superman battles it to travel fast. But he also needs it to walk or climb stairs. Friction happens whenever two things rub against each other. Rough surfaces cause more friction, smooth surfaces less. You can keep your balance walking across carpet. Walking on ice is trickier because there is less friction.

Pro athletes can't afford to let friction slow them down. Swimmers wear swimming caps to reduce drag from their hair. Many also shave their bodies to limit friction with water. Bicyclists shave their legs to fight friction caused by air resistance. Smooth legs help shave time off cyclists' races.

Competitive swimmers wear caps and shave their arms and legs to reduce friction in the water.

SLICK

Slicks give Formula One race cars extra grip on the road.

While athletes try to reduce friction, race car drivers crave it. Racers use tires called racing slicks. These tires may be smooth, but they create more friction than tires with treads. Since more of the tire touches the track, its grip is greater. The extra friction steals some speed from the car. But the slick's grip holds the car to the road on tight corners.

HOT BRAKES

Brakes on cars and airplanes use friction to reduce speed. This friction generates heat. Airplane brakes can reach temperatures of more than 1,800 degrees Fahrenheit (982 degrees Celsius). They must be cooled down before they can be used again.

AIR RESISTANCE

Superman's tight blue suit might do more than make him look good. His suit undoubtedly helps reduce friction with air molecules when he's flying. All moving objects encounter friction when they rub against air molecules. This friction is called air resistance or drag. The faster an object moves through the air, the greater its drag.

A meteor travels so quickly that it leaves a trail of smoke in its wake.

Really speedy objects, such as meteors, experience so much air resistance that they heat up. Meteors often enter Earth's atmosphere at 22,000 miles (35,400 km) to 157,000 miles (253,000 km) per hour. Friction with air molecules creates searing heat that burns up the rock, often before it ever hits the ground. When you spot a 'shooting star,' you are seeing flames from a burning meteor.

The spacecraft that carries the Curiosity Rover has a rounded bottom to help protect it during entry.

Spacecraft also heat up as they reenter Earth's atmosphere. To combat reentry heat, engineers design blunt-shaped spacecraft. The blunt shape pushes air so fast that it can't get out of the way. It forms a cushion of air that protects the spacecraft from flaring gases.

SPEED IN NATURE

Superman isn't the only being on Earth with the ability to reach incredible speeds. When it comes to the animal kingdom, he has a little competition.

RAPID LAND ANIMALS

If Superman is looking for a competitor in a foot race, a cheetah might be up for the challenge. Cheetahs are Earth's fastest land animals. A cheetah can accelerate from zero to 60 miles (97 km) per hour in just three seconds. With its amazing speed, it knocks down its prey before attempting a kill.

cheetah

FACT:

The sloth is the world's slowest animal with a top speed of 0.15 mile (0.24 km) per hour. It's so slow that algae grows on its fur.

The cheetah would win a race against any animal on Earth, including humans. But speed in the animal world isn't just about how quickly creatures move their legs. In fact some speedsters have no legs at all. Australia's death adder is one of the fastest striking snakes in the world. It strikes, injects venom, and returns to strike position in under 0.15 second. Without antivenin, 60 percent of this snake's strikes to humans are deadly.

death adder

FAST FLIERS

When Metropolis' citizens see Superman in flight, they sometimes mistake him for a bird. It's no wonder. Birds are fast fliers. The peregrine falcon is the fastest flier in the animal kingdom. When swooping to catch its prey, it travels up to 200 miles (322 km) per hour.

Next to the peregrine falcon, the diving speed of the Anna's hummingbird seems slow. It only reaches speeds of up to 60 miles (97 km) per hour during its dives. But this tiny flier actually moves 385 body lengths in one second, which makes it the fastest animal on Earth. By comparison, the peregrine falcon only moves 200 body lengths per second.

peregrine falcon

Anna's hummingbird

Even more amazing are the g-force stunts the Anna's hummingbird performs. G-force is the force felt by a body due to gravity. Standing still we feel 1 g—or gravity's normal pull. But on a speeding roller coaster, we feel greater g-forces when we're pushed against our seats. In fact, the world's fastest roller coaster produces 1.7 g's. And astronauts blasting into space often feel g-forces up to 8 g's. But pulling up from a dive, the Anna's hummingbird experiences 10 g's!

FACT:

Mosquitoes aren't fast fliers, but they have speedy wings. They beat their wings 500 times per second.

SPEEDY SWIMMERS

Superman's speed in not limited to sky and land. He's also a powerful swimmer when the need arises. But the Man of Steel isn't the only speedster in the sea.

The sailfish holds the title as the fastest mover in water. It can leap from the ocean at 68 miles (109 km) per hour. Since water is more than 700 times more dense than air, these jumps require tremendous effort. Leaping fish can achieve greater speed than swimmers because they speed up when launching into less dense air. Scientists aren't sure if the sailfish's large sail helps it move fast. But they have discovered that its scales create small vortexes that envelope the fish in a pocket of air, reducing drag in water.

A sailfish uses its unique fin for speed.

SAILFISH SUPERCAR

The McLaren P1 hybrid supercar's design is based on lessons learned from the sailfish. The car's air ducts are lined with scales similar to sailfishes'. The vortexes created cause more air to move through the engine. The resulting 17 percent increase of air creates a more efficient car.

The fastest swimming mammals in the ocean are dolphins. Among these the killer whale, which is actually a dolphin, reigns with speeds of 35 miles (56 km) per hour. Dolphins' tails are the key to their speed. The tail works like airplane wings to create speed-increasing lift.

3D SHARK SKIN

Sharks are some of the fastest swimmers in the ocean. Mako sharks can swim more than 60 miles (97 km) per hour. The secret to their speed is the tooth-shaped denticles on their skin. These spurs create tiny whirlpools around the shark that suck it through the water. Researchers have even created their own shark skin with a 3D printer. This skin could one day be used to reduce drag on airplane wings. It could also coat underwater robots to make them more efficient.

FAST FORCES OF NATURE

Superman uses his power of speed for the good of humanity. But speed has a destructive side as well. Just look to Earth's most powerful natural disasters to see speed at its worst.

A tornado tears through Oklahoma, a part of the country known as "Tornado Alley."

Tornadoes generate the highest wind speeds on the planet. To measure the destructive power of these swirling monsters, scientists use the Enhanced Fujita (EF) scale. This scale ranks tornadoes from EF-0 to EF-5. EF-0's cause light damage. EF-5's, with wind speeds of more than 200 miles (322 km) per hour, are the most destructive. These twisters leave total destruction in their wake. Buildings are leveled. Bark is torn from trees. Vehicles are crumpled into heaps of metal. The fastest recorded wind speed on the planet is 318 miles (512 km) per hour. It occurred inside a 1999 tornado that touched down in Oklahoma City.

A satellite image of a hurricane over the Atlantic

Tornadoes whip up extraordinary wind speeds that last for a matter of minutes. But hurricane winds last for hours. Hurricanes are fed by warm rising ocean air. They churn and gain strength over the ocean before making landfall with winds of up to 150 miles (241 km) per hour. On top of that, the ocean water they push ashore can cause massive flooding. With their relentless winds and storm surges, hurricanes are among the most destructive and costly disasters on Earth.

FACT:

On May 18, 1980, the volcanic eruption of Mount St. Helens caused the fastest avalanche ever recorded. Debris rushed down the side of the volcano at 250 miles (402 km) per hour. When the avalanche plunged into nearby Spirit Lake, it caused an 850-foot (260-m) tsunami.

HUMAN SPEED

Nature does its best to rival Superman's power of speed. But humans are drawn to that power too. Whether sprinting on foot or zipping around in high-tech machines, people are always looking for the fastest way to get from here to there.

AMAZING AUTOMOBILES

Superman doesn't need a car to speed him from place to place. But humans are always testing how fast they can travel on four wheels. These days, the fastest cars that can legally take to the highway are called supercars. The current supercar champion is the Hennessey Venom GT. On February 14, 2014, it accelerated from zero to 200 miles (322 km) per hour in just 20.3 seconds. At 270 miles (435 km) per hour, it edged out the Bugatti Veyron Super Sport's previous record by just 2 miles (3 km) per hour.

Hennessey Venom GT

While supercars command the highways, jet dragsters rule off-road. Jet powered dragsters are the fastest cars on Earth. One of the earliest jet dragsters was the Green Monster. It used a J-79 jet engine and axles from a 1947 Ford and a 1937 Lincoln. The Green Monster set three land-speed records between 1964 and 1965. Its best speed was 577 miles (928 km) per hour set on November 7, 1965.

The Green Monster on display at the Bornemouth Airfield in England in 1968.

WORLD'S FASTEST HUMAN

Jamaica's Usain Bolt is considered the fastest human in the world. The track star has broken the men's 100-meter world record three times. His fastest time, 9.58 seconds set in 2009, remains unbroken today. At top running speed, Bolt flies down the track at nearly 28 miles (45 km) per hour.

EXTRAORDINARY AIRCRAFT

Land-speed records are impressive. But when humans really want to crank up the speed, they mimic Superman by taking to the skies. The SR-71 Blackbird has a lot in common with the Man of Steel. It's sleek, powerful, and can outrun a bullet. The SR-71's speed record of 2,193 miles (3,529 km) per hour, set back in 1976, remains unbroken by any manned jet aircraft. During its 24-year career with the U.S. Air Force, no SR-71 was ever shot down. It flew so high and so fast that enemy missiles never threatened it.

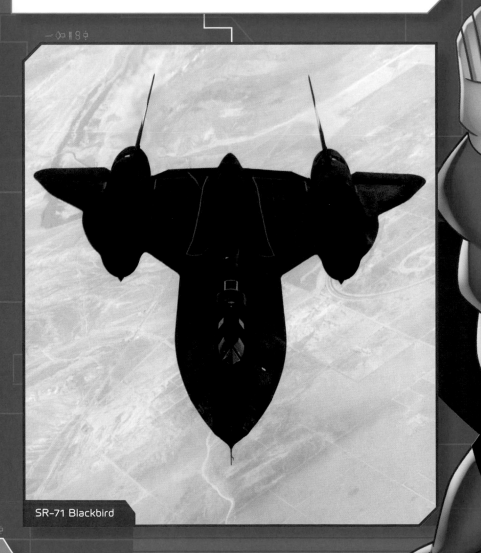

SR-71 Blackbird

North American X-15

Although not a jet plane, the experimental rocket aircraft, North American X-15, actually clocked a speed more than two times faster than the SR-71. At 4,520 miles (7,270 km) per hour, it holds the title as the fastest manned rocket plane. The X-15 was launched from the wing of a B-52 bomber. Each of its flights lasted only about 10 minutes. But they provided engineers with valuable information about aircraft performance at high altitudes and hypersonic speeds. X-15's successes laid the foundation for future space flight.

FACT:

Air resistance made the SR-71's cockpit windows so hot that pilots held their meals to the glass to cook them.

SPEEDY SPACECRAFT

The fastest inventions are those headed out of this world. Escaping Earth's atmosphere and traveling to the ends of the solar system require maximum speed. To break away from Earth, a spacecraft must travel 25,000 miles (40,000 km) per hour. This speed is called escape velocity.

Usually spacecraft speed is measured relative to the Sun instead of Earth. NASA's *New Horizons* holds the title of the spacecraft with the fastest launch speed. It launched in 2006 with a velocity of 100,000 miles (161,000 km) per hour. In 2015 it reached Pluto and continued onward to explore a region known as the Kuiper Belt.

an artist's rendition of the *New Horizons* spacecraft's encounter with Pluto

The *Helios I* and *II* solar probes until recently held the title of the fastest objects engineered by humans. Launched in 1974 and 1976, these probes entered orbits around the Sun. The Sun's mass caused them to reach orbital speeds of more than 150,000 miles (241,000 km) per hour.

A new record was set in 2016 by NASA's *Juno* spacecraft, which reached a max speed of 164,700 miles (265,000 km) per hour. In 2018 a new NASA spacecraft, *Solar Probe Plus*, will be launched. Its orbital speeds around the Sun will be 450,000 miles (724,200 km) per hour.

Engineers work on the *Helios II* solar probe prior to launch in the 1970s.

BRAIN SPEED

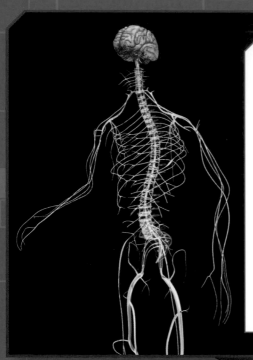

Superman's brain computes as fast as his reflexes, but your body is no slouch either. The center of your body's nervous system is your brain. It processes everything you see, hear, and feel. It tells your muscles what to do. Neurons are the speedy cells that carry messages from your body to your brain. Their transmission speed is 268 miles (431 km) per hour.

Neurons serve as the brain's messengers.

Your brain works with your eyes to make sense of what you see. Even when you're not aware of what you are seeing, your brain is. Researchers at Massachusetts Institute of Technology (MIT) discovered that your brain can correctly identify images that it sees for only 13 milliseconds. Most movie images are filmed three times slower. A movie flashes 24 frames per second, or one image every 42 milliseconds.

CHAPTER 4

STOPPING RUNAWAY TRAINS

SUPERMAN™ AND THE SCIENCE OF STRENGTH

HUMAN STRENGTH

Superman gets his strength by absorbing the energy from Earth's yellow Sun. But his muscles still work much like the ones in our bodies.

WHAT'S A MUSCLE?

Muscles are the parts of your body that create movement. They either move things inside your body, such as blood and food, or move the body itself. In fact your body has more than 600 muscles. They make up roughly 30 to 50 percent of your weight.

The three main types of muscles are smooth, cardiac, and skeletal. Smooth muscles are also called involuntary muscles. Why? Because they often move without you telling them to. Smooth muscles move food through your intestines, push air through your lungs, and even help your eyes focus.

Cardiac muscle is very specialized. It's only found in your heart. The heart is a muscle that pumps blood throughout your body. Just like some smooth muscles, it works all by itself with no help from you.

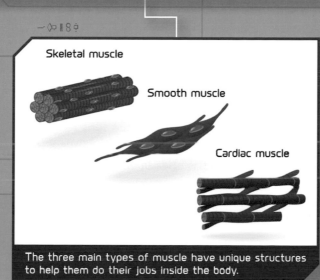

Skeletal muscle

Smooth muscle

Cardiac muscle

The three main types of muscle have unique structures to help them do their jobs inside the body.

The muscles you probably think about most are skeletal muscles. These can move, push, pull, and lift. Skeletal muscles are voluntary, which means they move the way you tell them to. They help you walk, run, throw a ball, and turn the pages of this book.

FACT:

Eye muscles are the busiest in the body. They may move more than 100,000 times a day.

THE MUSCULOSKELETAL SYSTEM

Skeletal muscles work with your bones to make up your musculoskeletal system. To provide power and strength, skeletal muscles must be connected to something solid to move your body. That something solid is bone. Imagine a runner pushing off a starting block to begin a race. Just like runners, muscles need a solid object on which to push or pull.

Most muscles are connected to bones by stiff, stringlike fibers called tendons. Some tendons are very long, allowing a muscle to move a bone that's far away. For instance, long tendons connected to muscles attached to your elbow help your fingers move. Other tendons are tiny, such as the ones in your ears and eyes.

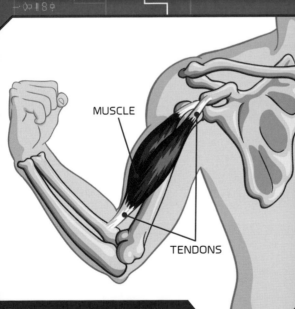

MUSCLE

TENDONS

Tendons connect muscles to bones.

FACT:

The biggest muscle in your body is the one you sit on. The gluteus maximus is just a fancy scientific name for your butt muscle.

Muscles cover your body in layers—and most bones have more than one muscle attached to them. The reason is simple. A single muscle can usually only work in one direction. You need multiple muscles to move in different directions.

Layers of muscles cover the body from head to toe.

MUSCLE SHAPES

Skeletal muscles come in many shapes and sizes to allow them to do different things. The muscles around your mouth are circular to allow it to open and close, whistle, or kiss. The deltoids in your shoulders are triangular. They need to be thicker where they attach to your shoulder blades. They are thinner where they attach to your arm.

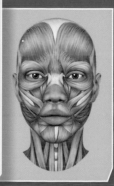

HOW MUSCLES WORK

When Superman keeps a skyscraper from toppling over, it's easy to be awed by his strength. But just like us, he has muscles under his skin. And whether muscles are superpowered or just human-powered, the science behind how they work is pretty remarkable.

Skeletal muscles are made up of fibers that line up next to each other in bundles. These muscle fibers contract and stretch, allowing your body to move. Contraction makes a muscle shorter. When a muscle gets shorter, it pulls on the bone attached to it.

Skeletal muscle

Consider the biceps on top of your upper arm, for example. This muscle attaches to the bones around your elbow and your shoulder blade. When you lift a glass of water, your biceps contract to pull your arm up. To put the glass down, you use the triceps located under your upper arm. This muscle contracts to lower your arm—and the glass—back to the table.

Tendon

Biceps
(relaxed)

Biceps
(contracted)

Triceps
(relaxed)

Triceps
(contracted)

The triceps and biceps work as a team to move your arm up and down.

BRAIN SIGNALS

How do your arm muscles know you want to lift an object? Your brain sends signals through nerves in the muscle fibers. The nerves tell the muscles to contract by sending electrical impulses. That's why an electrical shock makes your muscles twitch without you telling them to.

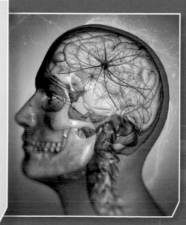

MUSCLE DISEASES

Just as Kryptonite can rob Superman of his strength, diseases can rob us of ours. Sometimes these diseases are caused by infections. Other times, people are born with them.

The tetanus vaccine has been widely used in the United States since the 1940s.

Tetanus is a disease caused by a type of bacteria usually found in dirt or soil. It affects the nerves that send messages to muscles. It causes extreme muscle spasms that can make it hard to breathe and can even break bones. Tetanus is also called "lockjaw." The disease can cause jaw muscles to tighten so much that victims can't open their mouths. But there's good news. The tetanus vaccine can prevent this disease.

Muscular dystrophy (MD) is a genetic disease some people are born with. It causes the muscles of the body to weaken and slowly stop working. Some children with MD use crutches, walkers, and leg braces to help them walk. Although there is no cure for MD yet, there are drugs and treatments that help slow the disease down.

Wheelchairs help people with muscle diseases gain mobility.

ENHANCING STRENGTH

Superman doesn't need to go to the gym to get huge muscles and incredible strength. Our yellow Sun's energy gives him the power boost he needs. For the rest of us, enhancing our strength takes exercise.

STRENGTH TRAINING

Regular exercise is great for your muscles, but it may not make you look like a super hero. For that you need strength training. This type of exercise uses resistance to make muscles work harder.

To feel how resistance makes your muscles work harder, try this simple test. Curl your arm while holding a small dumbbell. Can you feel your biceps working harder than normal? Now repeat the curling motion 10 more times. Is your arm getting tired? That means you're pushing your muscles to work harder. The more times you repeat an exercise, the harder your muscles must work. The harder they work, the stronger they become.

Dumbell curls strengthen the biceps.

Strength training can be done with your own body weight, resistance bands, free weights, and weight machines. Body weight strength training uses your own body's weight to create resistance. Common body weight exercises include push-ups, pull-ups, sit-ups, and leg squats. Resistance bands are long, lightweight bands that create resistance when you stretch them. Free weights include barbells and dumbbells. Weight machines have built-in weights or resistance bands to exercise specific muscles in the body.

Push-ups use the body's own weight to strengthen muscles in the arms.

MYOSTATIN AND MUSCLES

Almost every animal on Earth produces myostatin. This protein limits the size muscles can grow. But some animals, including mice and cattle, are born with a myostatin disorder. Their levels of myostatin are so low that they grow massive muscles without any strength training at all.

BODYBUILDING

Regular strength training is a good start to building a super hero body. But to really get the job done, weight training is the key. It's the type of strength training bodybuilders use to try to look as muscular as Superman.

Bodybuilders don't just build strength—they train specific muscles to maximize their size and shape. To do this, bodybuilders steadily increase the weight they lift as they train. These increases are necessary because muscles get used to exercise. If a bodybuilder always lifted the same weight, his or her muscles wouldn't get any bigger. But increasing the weight they lift actually causes tiny tears in their muscles. As their bodies repair these tears, bodybuilders' muscles bulk up.

Bodybuilders use weight training to sculpt their muscles.

FACT:

Actor and former California governor Arnold Schwarzenegger started out as a bodybuilder. He won titles at five Mr. Universe and seven Mr. Olympia bodybuilding competitions.

Bodybuilders use weight machines to help train specific muscle groups.

ANABOLIC STEROIDS

Our bodies make a hormone called testosterone that helps build muscle. Anabolic steroids are man-made versions of testosterone. Doctors sometimes prescribe these steroids to help people regain body mass after an illness. But some athletes, bodybuilders, and others take them illegally to increase muscle mass and strength. Anabolic steroid abuse can have extremely dangerous side effects including liver and heart problems.

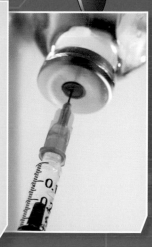

AEROBIC EXERCISE

Your heart is a muscle. While it can't lift weights, you can make it stronger by doing aerobic exercises.

The word "aerobic" means "with air." Aerobic exercise is any activity that makes you breathe more quickly and gets your heart pumping. Some examples include running, swimming, jogging, soccer, or dancing. It's basically any activity that makes you breathe harder and makes you sweat.

Aerobic exercise gives your heart muscle a workout.

Running and swimming both increase heart rate and build stamina.

When you do aerobic activities regularly, your heart gets better at its main job—delivering oxygen in the blood to the cells of your entire body. Your cells need oxygen to produce the energy they need to function. In addition, aerobic exercise helps you build endurance. That means you can stay active longer without tiring out as quickly.

FEATS OF STRENGTH

People have been fascinated by feats of strength for thousands of years. Long before Superman, Greek and Roman myths featured the tales of Hercules, the world's most famous strongman. It's no wonder, then, that modern feats of strength continue to capture our imaginations today.

WEIGHTLIFTERS

Some of today's most impressive feats of strength happen in the Olympic Games. Nowhere is this more true than in the sport of weightlifting, where men and women compete by hefting incredible weights above their heads.

Olympic weightlifters compete using two types of lifts: the clean-and-jerk and the snatch. The clean-and-jerk is made up of two movements. During the "clean," lifters move the barbell from the floor to their collarbones. During the "jerk," the lifters raise the barbell above their heads, with straight arms and legs. For the "snatch," the goal is to lift a barbell from the ground and overhead in one continuous motion.

clean-and-jerk

snatch

WEIGHTLIFTING RECORD-HOLDERS

Hossein Rezazadeh from Iran holds the current men's Olympic record for both the snatch and the clean-and-jerk. He lifted 467 pounds (212 kg) using the snatch. He hoisted 580 pounds (263 kg) using the clean-and-jerk. For women, Tatiana Kashirina of Russia holds the current Olympic record for the snatch at 333 pounds (151 kg). Lulu Zhou of China holds the clean-and-jerk record at 412 pounds (187 kg).

THE WORLD'S STRONGEST MAN

Olympic weightlifting isn't the only competition that pushes the limits of the human body. The World's Strongest Man competition tests competitors' strength with a variety of unusual events. Among them are the Farmer's Walk and the Atlas Stones.

In the Farmer's Walk, competitors carry two 353-pound (160-kg) weights. The goal is to move them a set distance within a certain amount of time. Competitors can set down and pick up the weights as many times as they like. But the one who completes the walk with the fastest time wins the event.

A strongman competitor prepares to lift two barbells in a Farmer's Walk event.

FACT:

In Greek mythology Atlas is a Titan who holds up the sky. During his adventures Hercules once held up the sky in Atlas' place.

The Atlas Stones event features five round stones. The lightest weighs 220 pounds (100 kg). The heaviest weighs 353 pounds (160 kg). Competitors need to pick up and place these massive stones on five high platforms on a 16- to 33-foot (5- to 10-m) course. The person who completes the course the fastest wins.

Atlas

ARM WRESTLING

In arm wrestling, winners and losers are decided by whose muscle fibers can fire simultaneously the fastest. The *Guinness Book of World Records* lists John Brzenk as the Greatest Arm Wrestler of All Time. He is known for easily pinning opponents twice his size. The heaviest opponent he defeated weighed 660 pounds (299 kg). That was more than twice Brzenk's weight.

HYSTERICAL STRENGTH

Every so often a news story appears that sounds like it was lifted from a Superman comic. In 1982 Tony Cavallo was pinned when the Chevy Impala he was working under fell off its jacks. Seeing her son in danger, Tony's mother lifted the car long enough for neighbors to pull Tony to safety. Similarly, in 2006 Tim Boyle saw a Chevy Camaro hit and pin a teenager underneath it. Boyle jumped into action and lifted the car to save the teenager's life. Neither Cavallo nor Boyle were strength competitors or weightlifters. How were they able to lift 3,000-pound (1,361-kg) cars in these moments of crisis?

In emergencies the human body has been known to perform unbelievable feats of strength.

Ordinary people who suddenly gain extraordinary strength, especially during life-or-death situations, are believed to experience hysterical strength. Gathering scientific evidence to prove hysterical strength exists is difficult, but scientists have theories about how it works. Our bodies produce adrenaline and noradrenaline in stressful and dangerous situations. These hormones raise heart rates and increase breathing. This allows blood to flow more easily to muscles, which delivers more oxygen to fuel them. These hormones also allow muscles to contract more than when the body is calm. Scientists think a sudden spike in these hormones during life-threatening events could produce surges of incredible strength.

ANIMAL STRENGTH

When super-villains wreak havoc on the world, Superman's incredible strength is often the difference between life and death. Strength plays an important role in how animals survive in their environments too. Large and small, animals flex their muscles in remarkable ways.

BIG AND STRONG

In the animal world, brute strength is all about size. You've probably heard the saying "strong as an ox." The phrase exists for a reason. Oxen are huge, making them the go-to work animal for thousands of years. An ox is so strong it can pull about one and a half times its body weight. A team of oxen working together can pull thousands of pounds. No wonder they were historically used to plow fields, haul wagons, and power machines to grind grain.

oxen

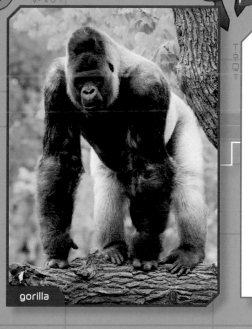
gorilla

Gorillas, the world's largest primates, are no slouches in terms of brute strength either. Males can be 5 feet 9 inches (1.75 m) tall and weigh 440 pounds (200 kg). They are believed to have about six times more upper body strength than an average man. A gorilla can lift objects that weigh 4,400 pounds (2,000 kg). That's 10 times its body weight!

Not to be outdone, Bengal tigers—the biggest members of the cat family—are known for impressive strength too. After a kill they often drag their meal to a hiding place. One Bengal tiger was seen dragging an adult gaur (similar to a bison) 40 feet (12.2 m). An average adult gaur weighs 2,000 pounds (907 kg)!

Bengal tiger

BIGGER AND EVEN STRONGER

Superman is famous for stopping runaway trains. But did you know some animals on Earth might have enough strength to do the same? In fact in the 1890s an elephant reportedly charged and derailed a train to protect its herd.

An elephant derailing a train is easy to imagine when you stop to consider its size. African elephants are the largest land animals on the planet. They can grow about 13 feet (4 m) tall at the shoulder and weigh up to 14,000 pounds (6,350 kg). An elephant that size can carry almost 20,000 pounds (9,070 kg). Even more impressive, an African elephant's flexible trunk has tens of thousands of muscles. It can lift 770 pounds (349 kg)—or the weight of three large men together—with its trunk alone!

African elephant

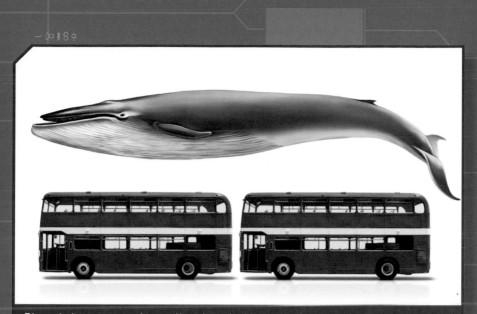

Blue whales can grow longer than two double-decker buses parked end-to-end.

Elephants may be the largest land animals, but blue whales are the largest animals to ever live on Earth. They measure up to 100 feet (30 m) long and weigh up to 200 tons (181 metric tons). That's longer than two double-decker buses end-to-end and as heavy as about 28 elephants! The muscles of such large animals can generate a huge amount of force. In 2014 a blue whale tipped over a 21-foot- (6.4-m-) long boat off the coast of California.

STRONG AND TINY

Amazing strength isn't limited to big animals. One of the strongest animals in the world for its size is the mantis shrimp. This 4-inch- (10-cm-) long sea creature packs a punch with the speed of a .22 caliber bullet. It uses its club-like body parts to break the shells of the crabs and snails it eats. When the shrimp releases its clubs, they accelerate to 50 miles (80 km) per hour. Where does all this power come from? The clubs are spring loaded, like a crossbow. Aquarium tanks have to be made of especially strong plastic because these tiny shrimp can actually shatter glass!

mantis shrimp

horned dung beetle

Mantis shrimp aren't the only mighty mini-creatures in the world. The strongest insect on the planet is the horned dung beetle. Yes, it feeds on dung—but what it can pull is even more amazing than what it eats for lunch. The horned dung beetle can pull 1,141 times its own body weight. That would be like a person pulling 180,000 pounds (81,650 kg), or six double-decker buses. That's one strong bug!

STRONGEST JUMPER

The tiny copepod is the world's strongest jumper. This crustacean is barely 0.04 inch (1 mm) long. But its jumping muscles are 10 times more forceful than any other animal's on Earth. A 5-foot 8-inch (173-cm) tall person leaping with the same power would top out at 3,800 miles (6,115 km) per hour!

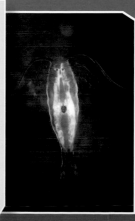

STRONG CHOMPERS

Superman isn't called the Man of Steel for nothing. He's as strong as steel and has been known to bend it with his bare hands. Turns out some animals might have the same abililty with their mouths!

The bird never had a chance against the jaws of this saltwater croc.

Bite force is measured in pounds per square inch (psi). The average person has a bite force of about 150 to 200 psi. That force allows us to chew through sandwiches and pieces of steak. Predators such as hyenas, lions, and tigers generate about 1,000 psi of bite force. This allows them to crush the bones of their prey. But the strongest bite force ever measured came from the saltwater crocodile. It can slam its jaws shut with a bite force of 3,700 psi!

While saltwater crocodiles have the strongest bite ever meausured, scientists think other animals may have even stronger bites. Computer models estimate the great white shark can bite down with 4,000 psi of force. And prehistoric animals may have had bite forces that were off the charts. The *T. rex* is believed to have had a bite force of 12,814 psi. And the *Deinosuchus*, or terrible crocodile, had a bite force estimated as high as 23,100 psi.

The jaws of the great white are so infamous that the movie *Jaws* was made about them.

STRONGEST TEETH

Crocodiles may have a strong bite, but limpets have the strongest teeth in the world. These small aquatic snails use their teeth to scrape algae off rocks. Their teeth's tensile strength— the amount of force it can take without breaking—is equal to a single strand of spaghetti holding 3,000 pounds (1,360 kg). Limpet teeth are the strongest known natural material on the planet.

FUTURE STRENGTH

People can only dream about having Superman's strength. But if scientists and engineers get their way, those dreams may one day become a reality. Check out the exciting ways science and technology might enhance strength in our world.

EXOSKELETONS

If you had Superman's X-ray vision, you'd see the skeletons inside people's bodies. But did you know some animals, such as insects and crustaceans, have skeletons on the outside of their bodies? These exoskeletons have inspired scientists and engineers with ways to boost human strength.

Human exoskeletons have already been developed for the military. Lockheed Martin's Human Universal Load Carrier (HULC) is designed to help soldiers carry heavy loads in combat. The HULC exoskeleton straps onto a soldier's thighs, waist, and shoulders. Once on, the weight of a soldier's gear is transferred to the device's titanium legs. The HULC allows users to carry up to 200-pound (91-kg) loads with very little stress on the body.

Robotic exoskeletons allow people to lift heavy loads with very little effort and a low risk of injury.

The HULC isn't the only exoskeleton being developed for the military. Raytheon Sarcos' XOS 2 is a full-body robotics suit for soldiers. It allows users to repeatedly lift 200 pounds (91 kg) of weight without getting tired. It's also strong enough to easily punch through 3 inches (76 mm) of wood. Engineers believe that one soldier wearing the XOS 2 can do the work of up to three regular soldiers.

MEDICAL MIGHT

The military isn't the only place where strength enhancement is the wave of the future. The medical field is also looking for ways to increase strength—both outside and inside the body.

While exoskeletons can help soldiers carry heavy loads, they can also help people who are paralyzed from the waist down. Ekso Bionics and ReWalk Robotics have already developed battery-powered exoskeletons for people with spinal cord injuries. These devices provide hip and knee motion to help people stand and walk. In 2012 a ReWalk helped Claire Lomas, who is paralyzed from the chest down, complete the London Marathon.

A battery-powered exoskeleton helps a woman walk.

Strength enhancement is also being studied on the microscopic level. Scientists hope to treat muscle diseases by changing the genes that cause them. In fact genetic engineering may change us more than any other technology in the future. For instance, scientists at Ohio State University and Nationwide Children's Hospital have changed a gene in macaque monkeys. It lets their muscles grow about 25 percent larger and stronger than normal.

macaque

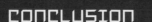
Some people might believe that superpowers are for super heroes only. But since the beginning of time, humans have strived to achieve bigger, better, faster skills—and tools to help us achieve what our anatomy hasn't been able to (yet!). From the days of the Wright Brothers to the future of interplanetary space travel, humans continually grasp at expanding our abilities and our world.

Drawing inspiration from our imaginations and nature, our powers are constantly improving. What once would have been considered science fiction or plain insanity (Laser surgery? Heat-seeking missiles? Titanium body parts? Trips to Mars?) is now reality. Superman's amazing abilities to stop on a dime mid-flight, to see through walls, or to soak up the power of the Sun reflect our limitless human imagination and the desire to use our own powers for good. Superman embodies our dreams to keep reaching for the skies.